Best Chicken Breeds: 12 Types of Hens that ~~~~~ ts, and Fit in Small Yards (Plus Bonus: 5 Varieties of Exotic Poultry) (36-page Booklet)

By R.J. Ruppenthal, Attorney/Professor/Garden Writer

- **How This Information Can Help You**

- **Rainbow Eggs: White, Blue, Green, Dark Chocolate Brown, and More**

- **Importance of Hatching Eggs and Handling Chicks Early**

- **Each Chicken is an Individual**

- **Best Breeds: 12 types of hens that lay lots of eggs, have friendly and calm temperaments, and fit in city backyards**

- **Bonus: 5 Exotic Poultry Chicken Breeds for backyards: wait 'till you see these!**

- **Resources Section: Links to additional information on chicken breeds, plus where to obtain your chickens**

Note on the Print Edition of this Booklet

This booklet originally was created as an e-book for the Kindle. By popular demand, I am releasing this print edition as well. The print version costs more because of the added production costs. Sadly, I had to make the decision (as I have with my other print booklets) to go with a black-and-white interior (as opposed to color). The colors in these pictures of the various chickens are so beautiful and they may even be important to you as you select which kinds of chicken you like best.

However, the break-even point for a color book of this length would be in the $8-$9 range and I don't want to charge people that much for such a short booklet. Therefore, consider this information (and the black-and-white pictures) a starting point and then go online to conduct a search for the name of any chicken breed you find interesting. You will see many more full color pictures online. Thanks for your understanding.

How This Information Can Help You

Thinking about getting chickens? Not sure what kind is best? If you're ready to learn which types of hens lay lots of eggs on a regular basis, make good pets, and fit happily in small sized yards, you've come to the right place. This e-booklet, which is a companion to my <u>Backyard Chickens for Beginners: Getting the Best Chickens, Choosing Coops, Feeding and Care, and Beating City Chicken Laws</u> (also available as an e-book or in print on Amazon), provides you with information on 12 types of chickens which are best suited for a small back yard flock. As a bonus, I've included 5 more breeds in the Exotic Poultry chapter at the end.

There's a lot of free information online about different kinds of chickens. It's great to have this available, but sorting through it can take a lot of time. When I decided to get chickens, I spent many hours researching different chicken breeds in books and on the Internet. At the time, I had a small yard in the city. The only thing I knew about chickens was that the hens lay the eggs and the roosters make most of the noise!

From my research, I learned that there are as many as 175 different kinds of chickens in the world. However, only 12 chicken breeds met my criteria, which were:

- Regular and prolific egg layers
- Comfortable in an enclosed coop and run area
- Preferably, not too loud
- Friendly around people

First, I only had enough space for 2-4 chickens, so it made sense to choose a kind that would lay lots of eggs. If a hen from Breed A lays an average of two eggs per week, while a Breed B hen averages four or five eggs per week, then why would I want Breed A? That's 100 eggs per year versus 200-250. If I'm feeding these birds and keeping them for egg production, then I want my chickens to be serious about laying. In this booklet, we will cover the most productive types of egg laying hens.

Second, I heard that not all chickens are comfortable in enclosed spaces like the cop and enclosed run area I was building. Some breeds are flighty and nervous, preferring to free range all the time, and often perching on fences and flying into trees if you let them out. But other chickens handle confinement well, remain happy in small spaces, and are likely to stay in a fenced yard when you let them out to free range.

I put the happy ones on my list. While I like to allow my hens to free range in the backyard, I cannot do this all day, every day. Like most of you, I have a day job and am away from home most of the day. When I am gone, our chickens stay in their coop and enclosed run area. When I'm home, I'll let them out into the yard. Getting them down from trees and chasing them through neighbors' yards is not how I want to spend my evenings. Unless you have a huge amount of space, choosing birds that can handle confinement is probably a wise bet for you, too. You will find them in this booklet.

Third, with a small city yard and neighbors close on every side, I wanted to find some quiet chickens. Roosters are the loud ones, and I had no intention of getting a rooster (which are not needed for egg production and are illegal in my city anyway). However, some hens crow a bit also, and this can be particularly loud in the morning or when they announce that they have laid eggs. There is always a chance of getting a loud chicken from any breed, but a consensus has emerged on which breeds are the quietest on a regular basis. This information took me the longest to find, but I will save you time by summarizing it in this e-booklet.

Finally, being friendly around people was not a "make or break" factor for me. But since I have two young kids, I thought it would be nice if the chickens could be pets also. This meant they would not run away from people. Hopefully, once they got used to their new home, they would allow us to approach them, feed them, and pick them up once in awhile. Again, the breeds covered in this book fit that definition.

It would take you at least two or three hours just to find this information, even before you sort through, read, and analyze it. Instead, I've put all the important stuff in this short booklet (which only appears longer because of all the chicken pictures, another essential element for people choosing breeds). In the text portions, I've summarized the lengthy raw material from my own research, selected the best breeds for backyards, and presented this information in a format you can use. Basically, it's the research and analysis I did for my own purposes and I'm passing it along to you.

If your time is valuable, then this short e-booklet will save you money. But if you prefer to do your own research, I sincerely wish you the best of luck with it. Others who may NOT benefit from this e-booklet are folks who have different reasons for getting chickens. For example, if you prefer to raise exotic varieties of chickens that do not lay much or if you plan to raise chickens primarily as meat birds, then you should look elsewhere.

I believe everyone else will benefit greatly from reading this short booklet. In particular, it makes a great supplement to my comprehensive beginner's guide to raising chickens, entitled Backyard Chickens for Beginners: Getting the Best Chickens, Choosing Coops, Feeding and Care, and Beating City Chicken Laws. While that book refers you to the proper sources of information to research chicken breeds, this one actually does that legwork for you. The only thing left to do is read.

Rainbow Eggs

Various breeds of chickens lay eggs of different colors and shades. These range from the bright white eggs we know from the supermarket to dark, chocolate brown. In addition, there are blue and green eggs, cream colored eggs, light brown eggs, and speckled eggs. Get a few different chickens and you won't need to dye any eggs for Easter!

Here are two pictures of rainbow eggs, the second set in a nesting box. The darkest brown ones are probably from Marans hens, while the blue and green eggs usually come from Ameraucana (Easter Egger) hens. In the profiles of each breed in this booklet, I have listed the colors that each type produces.

Quite honestly, my chickens have always laid more eggs than were promised. I think the egg laying estimates for hens for each breed are conservative. Happy chickens lay lots of eggs. You can keep them happy with clean water, a place to scratch in the ground (even if it's an enclosed run), and a good, varied diet. If you keep them happy, my guess is that you'll get more eggs than I've listed below for each of the breeds.

Hatching and Early Handling

Chickens you have hatched from eggs usually make the best pets. These birds get to know you as mom and dad rather than as a potential predator. Hens raised from chicks will be friendlier over the course of their lives than birds who first meet you when they are chicks or pullets. This is one good argument for buying hatching eggs rather than chicks or pullets, even though the incubation and care of young chicks requires a little more work.

Even if you get your chickens as chicks, handling them early will help them relate to you also. Pick them up, pet them, and let them get to know you. Chicks are born curious, but as they get older, that instinctual fear of the unknown kicks in. If you get chickens as pullets ("teenage" hens younger than one year old), you can get them to become more friendly over time, but they will never trust you the way chickens do when they learn that trust at an early age.

Each Chicken is an Individual

As any chicken expert will tell you, there are common features to every breed. Physical attributes are the most obvious, but these common features also extend to personality and behavior. However, chicken experts also agree that every bird is an individual and it is impossible to predict personality and behavior with complete accuracy.

While this book provides information on the general characteristics of each breed, we also need to contend with the luck of the draw. For example, if you ordered ten chicks of a particular breed from a hatchery, you might find that eight or nine of them grow into quiet birds (consistent with the nature of that breed), but it is possible that one or two of them may make a racket. You might have five birds of another breed which are supposed to be great layers, and it turns out that four are incredible layers. But the fifth one is a bit of a lemon; she just eats and sleeps.

One of the great things about keeping chickens is getting to know their individual personalities. Some will come right up to you and want to be picked up and touched, while others (even if they are nice birds) prefer to keep a little distance. Some like certain foods, while others won't touch them. Some like to lay eggs in nesting boxes, while others make their own nests on the floor of the coop. Occasionally, you'll get a good layer who also is broody and has to be kicked off the nest, while others just abandon their eggs to you as soon as they've been laid.

I have one chicken who is a daredevil. When I dump food, soil, or mulch/bedding into their run, or when I wash something with a stream of water from the garden hose, the others will scatter to avoid whatever is falling onto the ground. But one chicken stays there, even if things are falling on her head, and she does not mind getting wet. She is curious and wants to be the first to find out what I am putting into their area.

Most of these individual personality differences are fun. On rare occasions, a very broody, aggressive, or loud hen can be a real pain in the neck, and you may have to get rid of her. But in general, all of the breeds mentioned in this book are quite reliable and I think you will be happy with whichever ones you choose.

Best Breeds

Here are the best chicken breeds I have found for backyards, presented in alphabetical order. Both standard and bantam sized birds are available for most of these breeds. The size information I have provided for each one refers to standard breeds only. Also, bantams usually do not lay as many eggs.

The 12 Best Backyard Breeds (Presented Alphabetically)

Ameraucana (Easter Egger)
Australorp
Brahma
Cubalaya
Delaware
Orpington
Plymouth Rock (Barred Rock)
Rhode Island Red
Star (Sex Link)
Sussex
White Leghorn
Wyandotte

Ameraucana (Easter Egger) Overview

Ameraucana hens are the famous blue and green egg layers. Developed in the United States, the name means American-Araucana. Araucanas are Chilean birds known for their large ear tufts and for laying green or blue eggs, a gene which they apparently passed on to Ameraucana birds (though some think they got it from another South American source).

Not all Ameraucanas lay blue or green eggs. I have had five of these hens at various times; one laid white eggs, another green-brown olive eggs, and the others light blue eggs. I have heard that some even lay brown or pink tinted eggs. So be prepared that if you only get one or two of these birds, you are not guaranteed to get blue eggs (though blue seems to be their most common egg color).

Besides laying exotic looking eggs at an above average rate, these birds are sweethearts. They are quiet, trusting, and very easy to keep in small yards. In a mixed flock, the Ameraucana often becomes the owner's favorite. If you are looking for some chickens the kids will love, you cannot do better than these. Some varieties of Ameraucana have beards as well as ear tufts which makes them look like they are wearing muffs.

The Ameraucana is recognized by the American Poultry Association (APA), but the recognized breed must meet certain coloring requirements to be labeled an Ameraucana. Those that do not meet these standards are called "Easter Eggers" instead. Some hatcheries will sell "Ameraucanas" that are actually non-APA compliant and should properly be tagged as "Easter Eggers". But in practice, most of us do not worry about professional breeding standards as long as they keep laying those beautiful eggs!

Ameraucana Facts

Size

These are fairly light, medium sized birds. Hens weigh around 5 pounds.

Coloring

There are many variations: Black, Blue, Brown, Silver, Wheaten, White, and more. Most commonly, the hens have brown or gold-laced black feathers. The neck usually contains more black than the rest of the body.

Eggs

Ameraucanas/Easter Eggers are prolific egg layers, producing right around 5 eggs per week. Eggs, which are medium sized, can be blue, green, white, brown, or tinted pink.

Nature

These are calm and lovable birds. They make some of the best pets.

Notes

They have small ("pea") combs, which are less subject to frostbite than many other breeds, so Ameraucanas may be a good choice in cold climates. Here is a picture of some of my Ameraucanas, digging up and improving the soil in a raised bed.

Australorp Overview

Australorps are egg laying machines. Their friendly, docile nature also makes them great pets. If you are looking for a hen with both features, you simply cannot do much better than Australia's national breed.

Australorps are large, black birds with bright red combs and wattles, though strains of white and blue (slate gray) Australorps also exist. They were developed in Australia from Black Orpington stock (hence the name, which is short for Australian Orpington). Their genetic lineage also includes Minorca, Langshan, and White Leghorn. They were bred in Australia as a dual purpose breed (for eggs and meat), but their egg laying capabilities quickly made headlines.

In the 1920s, a group of Australorps set a world record by producing an average of 309.5 eggs in the course of a year. A single Australorp hen later set an individual record by producing 364 eggs in 365 days. What may have been a regional or national breed was quickly shipped all around the world. Today, Australorps are fairly common in backyards and easy to find locally.

Australorp Facts

Size

Large hens range from about 7-9 pounds

Coloring

Generally: Jet black feathers and bright red combs and wattles. Feathers have an iridescent green or violet sheen in bright sunlight.
Blue: Slate gray feathers, usually with a darker neck.
White: Plumage is all white.

Eggs

Hens lay at a prolific rate, usually 5 eggs per week. Eggs are large and brown.

Nature

Friendly, quiet, and docile.

Notes

If you have a mixed flock, these birds usually get along quite well with other types of chickens. Here is a picture of a typical Australorp hen followed by a shot of an Australorp chick.

Brahma Overview

Brahmas are some of the biggest chickens around. Their heavy size means they will not be flying over many fences. They have some of the calmest, most easygoing personalities of any backyard chicken. This is probably one reason they have developed a devoted following of loyal fans around the world.

Brahma hens lay eggs at an average clip, but are not even close to being egg laying champions. The reason I have included them on this list, aside from their other outstanding attributes, is that Brahmas lay most of their eggs between October and May. In the coldest part of the year, when other laying hens are slowing down, Brahmas can be counted on to provide a steady source of winter protein. These cold hardy birds are a great choice for Northern climates, but not as good for the South.

In 1846, a shipment of chickens arrived in New York from Shanghai, China. These chickens may have originated in southern China, India, or somewhere in between. The birds arriving in this shipment may have been the Chinese breed now called Cochins, which were bred later with some birds from India to produce Brahmas, or else they may have been Brahmas when they arrived.

Whether they were developed in the United States or before they arrived here, Brahmaputras (later shortened to Brahmas) became a very popular chicken breed in the 19th Century. This popularity was due partly to the gift of a small flock to Queen Victoria, which solidly put Brahmas on the map (and netted the breeder who made the gift a much higher price for his birds). Today, there are Brahma chicken clubs in many locations, though the breed is less common than most others on this list. The American Poultry Association recognizes Brahmas. Dark, Light, and Buff are the three standard types, while more extreme red, black, brown, and other color types exist also.

Here is a picture of a light (nearly white) Brahma hen. There is a chick in the background also, which may be harder to see.

Brahma Hen Facts

Size

Very large, hens 10-14 pounds.

Coloring

Dark type: Mottled white on black.
Light type: Mostly white with black-striped collar.
Buff type: Tan with black-striped neck and mottled overlay.
Other types include: predominantly red, black, brown, and other colors. Roosters and hens of this breed can look very different.

Eggs

Hens lay at an average rate, usually producing 3 or more eggs per week. Eggs are brown and average in size.

Nature

Tend to be quiet, gentle, and easily habituate to confinement.

Notes

Brahmas have small combs and feathered legs. They are ideal for colder climates, but not warm ones. Because of their feathered legs, they may not be a good choice in muddy locations.
Here is a picture of a Brahma rooster. Unless you have an older monochrome Kindle (like mine), then you can see how much the coloring varies within this breed. This rooster looks much different from the hen in the previous picture. Both are beautiful birds and have those distinctive feathered legs.

Cubalaya Overview

Here is an unconventional choice that does not appear on most peoples' lists. Cubalayas do not appear in many backyards either, but they are spreading as they gain favor for their good looks, egg production, and calm demeanor. Several hatcheries sell Cubalaya chicks and I have seen ads for breeders who sell hatching eggs or chicks as well.

The breed was developed in Cuba from Asian stock which probably originated in the Philippines. These chickens are tame, peaceful, and make great pets as well as being great egg layers. They can handle confinement well. Cubalayas are still more popular in Cuba than elsewhere, but they have a devoted following.

Besides the attributes I've already mentioned, Cubalayas also make great show birds. The roosters are stunningly gorgeous and can hold their own with any game bird. They have bright colors which usually include bright red and black, plus a long, flowing lobster tail. The hens are much less colorful, but have a regal, upright bearing and that same angled tail. Here are pictures of both sexes.

Cubalaya Facts

Size

Medium sized, with hens reaching 4-5 pounds.

Coloring

Black Breasted Red: Roosters look like the previous picture with dark red necks and backs. Their bodies and tails are black with an iridescent sheen.
White: Usually same black portions as above with white neck and back.
Black: Plumage is all black.
Hens: Most commonly have dark cinnamon necks with a light cinnamon, tan, or wheaten body, and some black or gray tail feathers. Some can have lighter colored necks than bodies.

Eggs

Laying hens can produce quite well, around 4 eggs per week. Eggs are cream or tan in color.

Nature

Tame and peaceful for the most part (see notes below).

Notes

While most Cubalayas are calm and friendly around people, they can be aggressive toward other birds. Roosters are especially nasty and have been used for cockfighting in Cuba. If you plan to keep other chicken breeds as well, this may not be a good addition to your mixed flock. But if you plan to keep only this one breed, they should perform very well in your backyard.

Delaware Overview

Delaware chickens tend to be quiet and friendly, lay plenty of eggs, and tolerate small living areas well. This breed originated in 1940 and is a cross between New Hampshire and Barred Rock chickens. Delawares were developed as a dual purpose bird (for egg laying and meat), so they are good sized, yet produce eggs at an above average rate.

Delaware chickens are almost completely white with a touch of barred black striping on their necks and tail areas. While they are cold hardy, these birds do have a prominent comb. In cold winter climates, their combs should be rubbed with petroleum jelly to prevent frostbite.

During the middle of the 20th century, the Delaware became the most popular breed of broiler chicken on the East Coast. At that time, nearly every meat bird was raised in the state of Delaware, and most of them were its namesake breed. A few years later, Cornish crosses came into favor as meat birds and the Delaware faded.

Today, the bird is considered an endangered heritage breed. It is unfortunate that they're not more popular, because many Delaware owners consider them a perfect overall bird for backyard flocks. They are some of the friendliest and quietest chickens around, plus they lay lots of eggs.

Delaware Facts

Size

Medium, hens 6-8 pounds, averaging 6.5 pounds each.

Coloring

Mostly white with black barring on neck and tail.

Eggs

Lays at above average rate of 4-5 eggs per week. Eggs are large and brown.

Nature

Friendly and quiet.

Notes

Hatcheries have them, but Delaware chickens are less common than most others on this list. Therefore, finding them locally may be difficult.
Here is a picture of a Delaware hen.

Orpington Overview

Orpingtons are huge, block shaped birds that provide a good rate of egg production. They have dual purpose characteristics, often used for meat as well, making them a good fit for small farms. Orpingtons are very friendly and easygoing, so they have become favorites in backyard flocks also. To top it all off, they are quite cold hardy, which makes them suitable for northern climates.

The breed was developed in England in the late 19th century, putting the town of Orpington on the map. The original breeder reportedly created a black bird that would not show the soot of London. Today, the black variety still exists, as do white, blue, buff, and splash. Buff Orpingtons are the most popular, probably the world's most common blonde chickens.

Here is a picture of three Orpy hens in different colors: splash white, blue (gray), and buff.

Orpington Facts

Size

Very large, with hens ranging from 8 pounds to 10.5 pounds.

Coloring

Colors are predominantly solid, but soft and creamy, as you can see from the previous picture. Buff is the most common, but black, blue, white, and splash are others that also exist.

Eggs

Dependable layers of 3-5 eggs per week, which are large and brown.

Nature

Friendly, easygoing, not aggressive.

Notes

1) Orpingtons are nice enough that they're are often at the bottom of the pecking order in a mixed flock. 2) Hens should continue to lay through the winter, unlike many others.

Plymouth Rock (Barred Rock) Overview

No, they did not come on the Mayflower, but Plymouth Rock chickens have been around in New England since the mid 19th century. Created as a dual purpose (for eggs and meat) bird, Plymouth Rocks make a great small farm or backyard bird. They are calm, easygoing, and generally lay eggs at an above average rate.

Plymouth Rocks have several different coloring schemes, but the most popular is the black and white barred pattern. For this reason, many Plymouth Rocks are called Barred Rocks, and you will also hear the term Barred Rock applied to this entire breed. However, there are white, buff, black, silver, and other colors of Plymouth Rock chickens that do not have the full barring pattern and probably should not be called Barred Rocks.

Here is a picture of a Barred Rock hen. You can see a little Eglu coop in the background.

Plymouth Rock (Barred Rock) Facts

Size

Hens range from 6.5-7.5 pounds, making them one of the heavier breeds.

Coloring

Barred Rock: Black and white bar pattern with bright red combs and wattles.
Partridge: The partridge variety is dark red with a copper colored collar and some black feathers on the edges.
White (all white), black (all black), and several other color schemes exist as well.

Eggs

Very good egg layers (average about 4 per week), which are large and brown.

Nature

Calm, docile, easygoing.

Notes

It seems that some strains of Rocks are better layers than others. All are dependable, but some approach excellence in this department. Try to find out if yours comes from a good line with a productive history.

Rhode Island Red Overview

The Rhode Island Red (RIR) is one of the oldest standard American breeds. They are a large breed with dark red plumage, though a white variety also exists. Originally developed around 1840, the RIR is a dual purpose (for eggs and meat) bird. Today, it is not much used for meat because of its dark colored feathers, which tend to leave spots. But it remains a reliable layer of brown eggs.

Ask people to imagine a chicken and many of them will think of a RIR. This is the classic brick red chicken with a rectangular, brick shaped body. While the breed is not as popular as it once was commercially, it is one of the most common varieties of backyard chickens. RIRs lay lots of eggs with a low-key demeanor that keeps them popular. However, owners do report that these hens can be hot tempered and a little standoffish at times, an attitude that should mellow with time and familiarity around people.

The RIR is the state bird of Rhode Island. Bred to withstand cold New England winters, this is one of the hardiest breeds around. Also, they are said to tolerate close living conditions and marginal diets better than other chickens. I do not recommend you overcrowd your birds or feed them anything less than the best available food, but occasionally when you make a change or introduce something new into their diet, some breeds have a hard time adapting. These ones can handle it.

Rhode Island Red Facts

Size

Large birds are on the light side of heavy, with hens averaging 6.5 pounds in weight.

Coloring

Dark, brick red plumage with single red comb. Roosters have some dark green tail feathers also. A white strain exists, but is much less common.

Eggs

RIRs are frequent (5 eggs per week) layers of large brown eggs.

Nature

These redheads can be hot tempered, but usually gentle and low key.

Notes

Many people keep RIRs in a mixed flock and report no problems. However, a few owners report that these normally gentle birds can be aggressive around other birds. With a mixed flock, the easiest way to create harmony (aside from skipping the roosters) is to bring in the birds at the same time. Late introductions into an established pecking order can result in political issues. Below are pictures of RIR hens and a chick at nine days old.

Star (Sex Link) Overview

Increasingly popular are the hybrid chickens known as Red Star (Gold Buff), Black Star, or Gold Star. The Stars are also known as Sex Link chickens because their gender can be determined from the color of their feathers at the time they hatch. These are not officially recognized breeds, but they happen to be some of the most prolific egg layers and they make great pets also.

Most of us (non-professionals) are not able to determine the sex of newly hatched chicks, whose gender characteristics do not emerge until after several weeks of growth. But when you order chicks from a hatchery, you can order one day old female, male, or straight run (not sexed) chicks. Hatcheries employ professionals who are able to "sex" new chicks by performing a test on them. This test usually involves squeezing the poop out of them and seeing if they have a bump which indicates whether they are boys or girls (do not try it at home). As you can imagine, there is a higher demand for future egg layers than for future roosters.

However, through breeding, several crosses have been developed that produce different colored feathers for boys and girls. This makes it easier and more economical to sort these Sex Link chickens right away. Hatcheries have different formulas for these breeds, so there is no set standard. The two most common are called Red Star and Black Star, with Gold (or Golden) Star being available at some hatcheries also. In Europe, there are at least two other kinds as well. Stars are excellent egg layers and are reported to be some of the friendliest birds by their owners.

Star (Sex Link) Facts

Understandably, since hatcheries use different crosses, the breed characteristics can vary.

Size

Usually medium to large, with hens weighing around 5-6 pounds.

Coloring

Red Stars: Cinnamon, usually lighter than a Rhode Island Red. Plumage can have patches of white or light red feathers.
Black Stars: Jet black plumage, often with some dark red feathers around the neck.
Gold Stars: Buff or tan, often with cinnamon overlay.

Eggs

Very prolific layers of large brown eggs (5 per week is a good estimate).

Nature

Stars tend to be friendly, curious, and easygoing.

Notes

Some of the best egg layers and pets. They are winter hardy also. Here is a picture of some Red Stars in the snow.

Sussex Overview

The Sussex is an old breed of chicken originating in what is now the county of Sussex in South East England. Some say they have existed since the time of the Roman invasion while other reports have them being developed in the 1800s. Sussex hens are respectable egg layers and bring a calm, complacent manner to the backyard. At the same time, many Sussex owners have described these birds as the most active, alert, and intelligent of their chickens.

If you have space to free range your birds, this breed is a great bet. They are excellent foragers and can find most of what they need to eat, cutting down on your cost of supplementary feed. While they are not champion egg layers, they score a strong B+ for egg production.

Sussex chickens have blocky, rectangular bodies. They come in many different colors, including White, Buff, Brown, Red, and Silver. Most popular is the Speckled Sussex, which has dark brown and black feathers with contrasting white or light gray spots on its feather tips. Over time, speckled Sussex birds actually become more speckled as they molt and grow new feathers. Here is a picture of one.

Sussex Facts

Size

Hens are large, averaging around seven pounds.

Coloring

White, Buff, Brown, Red, and Silver and other colors exist. Speckled Sussex variety has white feather tips over dark brown or black plumage.

Eggs

Sussex hens lay large, light brown tinted eggs at a reliable rate of about 4 per week.

Nature

Gentle, calm, alert.

Notes

Speckled Sussex hens have a great camouflage against daytime predators, such as hawks, who may attack chicks and young pullets in the yard.

White Leghorn Overview

Leghorns are probably the most common commercial egg layers. They may not be the nicest, cuddliest breed on this list. A few owners have described them as flighty and edgy, while others swear that their Leghorns are nothing but calm and tame. But these Italians lay almost as many eggs as there are days in the year, so they are worth at least a look.

Due to Leghorns' unreliable temperament, I may be stretching things a bit to put them on this list. But if you are less concerned with a cuddly pet and just want a bird that can handle backyard confinement while laying huge numbers of eggs, then Leghorns are still a good choice. Hatching them from eggs or handling chicks at an early age may improve their social skills around people. Leghorns are named for the city of Livorno (Leghorn in English) in Tuscany, Italy. Leghorns were developed near the horn on Italy's geographic boot and first exported in 1828. Since then, they have become a commercial success. Breeders have continued to refine the breed's characteristics and use it to bring prolific egg laying qualities to other crosses.

White Leghorn Facts

Size

Medium sized breed, with hens reaching 4.5-5.5 pounds.

Coloring

White, black, and brown are the original standard colors, but today there are more than a dozen variations. Most commonly, the birds are all white with pink combs and wattles.

Eggs

They lay huge quantities of big, white eggs. The typical white eggs you see in the supermarket were probably produced by Leghorns.

Nature

It seems to vary with the bird. They can handle confinement and generally do well in backyards. But some owners see them as nervous and edgy, while others describe their Leghorns are calm and tame.

Notes

1) White Leghorns can lay as many as 300 eggs per year. Other colors of this breed may turn out to be less prolific, since they have been bred for their looks rather than egg production. 2) These birds can have large, droopy combs (some seem to have larger ones than others). In wintertime,

keep these areas from getting frostbitten by rubbing them with petroleum jelly. Note the floppy combs in the following picture of a Leghorn flock.

Wyandotte Overview

These birds are longtime backyard favorites. Wyandottes lay quite well, handle confinement without complaint, and have a calm, carefree nature. They are dual purpose breed, having good value as both egg layers and meat birds.

Wyandottes were developed in the United States, probably in New York in the late 1800s. Most people find them quite attractive, since they tend to have swirled or spotted color patterns due to the dark highlights on the edges of their feathers. Many different colors exist and the highlighted edges on feathers are known as "lacing". For example, a Gold Laced Wyandotte has predominantly gold feathers that are outlined in black, which does look a lot like lacing or netting. Here is a picture of one, so you can see what I am talking about.

Wyandotte Facts

Size

Medium to heavy birds, with hens weighing around 6-6.5 pounds.

Coloring

There are many different colors of Wyandottes. These include black, white, and buff, as well as gold laced, silver laced, and partridge (with a golden collar).

Eggs

Wyandottes are great layers of large, brown eggs, averaging about 4 per week.

Nature

Calm and carefree, very accepting of confinement.

Notes

While they are calm birds, they often run the show from the top of the pecking order, keeping other birds in line. Also, they are not quiet, since they cluck a lot, but they aren't usually too loud either.

Conclusion

I hope this information in this booklet has been helpful to you in deciding which kind of chickens to get for your backyard flock. It was just the information I needed when I first set out to learn about different breeds. I found all the right information, but it took me much longer than this to sort through the material and pick out the best breeds for my needs. Since I suspect that most people want the same things: good egg layers that are nice and fit in backyards, I put this information together here. So I hope this booklet has not only educated you, but that it will save you some time as well.

To recap, if you want champion egg layers, Australorps are the top choice. The next best layers are probably Red Stars (Gold Buffs) and Black Stars, followed by White Leghorns and Ameraucanas. If you just stuck to that list, you would have some brown, white, and blue/green eggs! But many of the other members of the list I've covered also lay respectably and make terrific additions to your backyard. Again, if you want a great overall guide to raising chickens for beginners, I highly recommend Backyard Chickens for Beginners: Getting the Best Chickens, Choosing Coops, Feeding and Care, and Beating City Chicken Laws, which is available on Amazon.

Finally, following the bonus section below, there is a short Resources section. This provides you with links to the Internet sources I used for my own research. Now that you have a basic overview of the best backyard chicken breeds, you get more information on any one of them from these sources. The Resources section also contains links on where to obtain chickens.

Can I ask you a Quick Favor?

Dear Reader,

I hope you have enjoyed this e-booklet and learned something useful. Once you are finished reading, I have a brief favor to ask. Please leave a short review of this book on Amazon to help future readers. Thank you! –R.J. http://www.amazon.com/dp/B008JI3M6O

Bonus Section: Five Exotic Poultry Chickens

Some other good chicken breeds did not quite make the cut for the top 12 above. For example, Faverolles, Welsummers, and New Hampshires all make good backyard birds as well; they are pretty decent egg layers and fairly nice to be around. But as I ruled out a few other breeds, it occurred to me that several exotic types had come close to meeting my criteria as well.

These five, Marans, Turkens, Polish (with the feather duster hairdo in the previous picture), Silkies, and Serama Chickens are so cool that each one deserves some special mention. None of them can boast the prolific, reliable egg production of the 12 breeds recommended above, but all of them make pretty good pets, and both Marans and Turkens hens are respectable egg layers. The other three, Seramas, Silkies, and Polish, are basically bantam sized birds, so even though some lay well, it may take a couple of weeks to get enough eggs for an omelet.

Marans Overview

We'll start the exotic list with Marans, which lay the beautiful dark brown eggs in the picture above. French and English Marans chickens are exotic, but not because of their appearance. They are beautiful birds to look at, but this alone does not make them unusual, since many chickens are attractive birds. Marans qualify as exotic because they lay chocolate eggs.

Do the eggs taste like chocolate? Unfortunately not, but their coloring is as dark brown as any cocoa. The darkest brown eggs are produced by Black Copper Marans hens (making them highly sought after), while Silver Cuckoo Marans hens (which are more common in the U.S.) also produce a very dark egg.

The Marans breed was developed in France, where both its fine white flesh and dark brown eggs were favored by chefs. In 1929, some hatching eggs were smuggled into Britain, and further breeding took place in both countries. Today, there are a lot of Marans crosses as well as several standard colors for the breed. The hens lay at a reasonable rate. Most Marans are calm and interested in people, though personalities can vary a great deal within the breed. Here is a picture of a Marans hen (in the foreground) with some adopted chicks that she mothered.

Marans Facts

Size

Hens 6-7 pounds.

Coloring

Black copper, silver, cuckoo (black and white spotting or barring, like Barred Rocks), golden, white, blue, wheaten.

Eggs

Hens are good layers of around 3 eggs per week, which are large and very dark brown.

Nature

Mostly calm and personable, but some variation.

Notes

Black Copper Marans that meet the French standard are quite rare in the U.S., where this class of chicken has not been officially recognized yet. At the same time, a lot of mixed breeds exist, which sellers may pass off as being genuine Black Copper Marans. If you see an advertisement for hatching eggs, make sure the seller mentions that they meet the French standard. If you are offered some Marans chicks or pullets, they must have feathered legs to be the real French article, or else they are probably British crosses. For some reason, the British breeding resulted in featherless legs. Of course, you may actually want birds without feathered legs, which are easier to keep clean.

Turken (Transylvanian Naked Neck) Overview

Take a look at the picture below. What kind of bird is this?

With a featherless neck and floppy wattles, the Turken resembles a turkey cross from the neck up. In fact, it is all chicken. Turkens (also called Naked Necks) were developed in Central Europe. They probably were bred for the featherless feature with the goal of producing a bird that would tolerate hot weather.

Turkens are calm, docile, and handle confinement well. Some owners have tried them because of their unusual looks and ended up falling in love with them as pets.

Turken (Transylvanian Naked Neck) Facts

Size

Hens average 6.5 pounds

Coloring

Turkens can be white, black, buff, or red.

Eggs

Figure on 3 eggs per week and maybe more, light brown.

Nature

Calm, docile, smart, and friendly.

Notes

I couldn't think of a good Dracula joke. These guys are spooky enough on their own.

Polish Chicken Overview

Polish are one of the most unusual looking breeds of poultry. Their crested heads resemble feather dusters or something from an 80's metal band. In addition to their crests, some Polish varieties are bearded as well. This breed is frequently used for show birds. While suitable as pets and moderate egg layers, their main attraction is their exotic appearance and resulting entertainment value.

Polish chickens are calm, cooperative, and do not mind sticking to small areas if confined. Most hens lay fewer eggs than average, but some owners report a higher rate of egg laying. With the feathers on their heads, they cannot see all that well, so they frequently appear to behave strangely. In the backyard, they are fun to watch and make great conversation starters for all your backyard cocktail parties.

Despite the name, these chickens are not Polish. They probably entered Europe from the east, so someone thought they had come from Poland. The breed probably originated in Asia and was spread by the Mongols. Its first mention in historical texts was in the 16th century. However, an archaeological dig at a Roman site in Britain turned up the skull of a bird that perfectly fit today's Polish chicken. So this may be one of the oldest breeds in existence today.

Polish Chicken Facts

Size

Small, hens 4-5 pounds.

Coloring

Golden, silver, white, buff, white crested black, and black crested white.

Eggs

Usually 2-34 eggs per week from laying hens, which are bantam sized white eggs.

Nature

Calm, cooperative, accepting of a small area.

Notes

Please don't use your birds to clean cobwebs on the ceiling. If I didn't say it, someone would complain that I promote animal cruelty! Here is another picture of a Polish chicken (the picture at the beginning of this "Five Exotic poultry Chickens" section also showed a Polish).

Silkie Overview

It's a bunny, a kitten…no, it's a chicken! Silkies are unusual birds in that they have soft, downy feathers. These feathers resemble fur or silk. Their calm, peaceful nature also makes them excellent pets.

Silkies originated in Asia, probably in China or Southeast Asia. They were mentioned by Marco Polo in his accounts of his travels in the Orient. In Asia, their black fleshed meat is exotic as well, purported to help people with diabetes, anemia, and weak immune systems.

Silkies lay eggs consistently. However, remember that these are very small eggs, so even if you get three per week from a hen, that may not be enough to equal one standard sized egg. Here is a Silkie picture (yes, that's the head, and yes, they do have bright blue ears).

Silkie Facts

Size

Standard hens are 3 pounds. Believe it or not, there is a smaller bantam version also.

Coloring

White, black, buff, blue (gray), and other colors.

Eggs

Good rate of 3 per week, cream colored and bantam sized.

Nature

Calm, relaxed, make good pets.

Notes

Despite their lightweight size, Silkies do not fly well, so even a 3-foot fence should contain them.

Serama Overview

This guy looks as cocky as any rooster, but he is less than one foot tall.

Serama chickens are a miniature bantam breed. Developed in Malaysia, the Serama lays claim to being the world's smallest chicken. Full grown roosters (like the one in the previous picture) top out at about one pound in weight, give or take a few ounces. They can fit in smaller than normal spaces, not needing as much room in a coop or run and eating a lot less food than larger birds.

In addition to the novelty of their size, Seramas hold their tails at an unusually acute angle that makes them unique. They are friendly, easy to handle, and get along well with other chickens. But some owners have reported their Seramas can get loud, while others label them as very quiet pets.

This is a fairly new breed, so it is not yet widespread. The birds are very popular in Malaysia, where Serama shows are held every weekend. In the United States, they are gaining popularity, particularly as pets for people who have limited space. Here is a picture of a Serama hen; the resolution is poor, but you can see that she holds her tail as the same angle as that rooster in the previous image.

Serama Facts

Size

Hens are less than one pound in size. Seramas measure from 6-10 inches tall.

Colors

In Malaysia, these chickens have not been bred for their color, but for other characteristics. As a result, most birds have lots of patchy reds, blacks, and whites on their plumage.

Eggs

Hens lay miniature eggs up to half a pound in weight. They can be white, dark brown, or any shade in between. Frequency for laying hens can approach 3-4 eggs per week. Roughly 5 Serama eggs = 1 standard egg.

Nature

Very calm and accepting of human contact. Great pets.

Notes

These are warm weather birds, which should not be outside when temperatures fall below 40 degrees. Some people keep them as indoor pets.

Reminder: Please leave a short review of this booklet!

Dear Reader,

I hope you have enjoyed this booklet. Please take a moment to leave a brief review on Amazon, letting other readers know what you think. Just a few words would be appreciated. Thanks! –R.J. http://www.amazon.com/dp/B008JI3M6O

Resources

My main sources for this booklet are as follows. They provide much more information on chickens. Each one is a valuable resource.

Great information and unbeatable forums. Many other chicken owners posted valuable advice on breeds which was helpful in understanding their egg laying and personalities: http://www.backyardchickens.com

Another helpful forum where poultry owners share information: http://poultrycommunity.com

And this British forum site is also valuable: http://forums.thepoultrykeeper.co.uk/index.php

Various information on chickens and chicken supplies: http://www.mypetchicken.com

Wikipedia and Wikimedia Commons, the source of some of the information on various breeds and many of the images appearing in this booklet: http://www.wikipedia.org

Rare Breeds of Chickens: http://blog.mcmurrayhatchery.com/2011/02/09/rare-breeds-of-chickens

American Poultry Association (includes list of recognized breeds and show information): http://www.amerpoultryassn.com

Getting Chickens

1. Local Pullets. If you are buying pullets (young hens almost ready to lay), then it is best to look locally first. Try your regional Craigslist site, and look under the "For Sale" category for the "Farm+Garden" link and local classified ads. You can try a key word search for "chickens" or "hens" or "pullets" or "chicks" too. Alternatively, ask at your local farm supply or feed store, which may sell chickens or know who else does. Or you can post your own ad on here explaining what you are looking for, using a blind e-mail address. You never quite know what

you are getting from a classified site, but most people (though not all) are honest and good. www.craigslist.org

2. Buy/Sell/Trade/Free. Some online poultry forums have organized threads for sales and barter. One good one is Chicken Chatter, which has a forum called Buy/Sell/Trade/Free. Last time I looked on there, one poster was selling hatching eggs for several varieties for $8-24, depending on the breed, while someone else was trying to find some French Copper Marans chicks (Copper Marans are famous for laying the most beautiful dark chocolate-colored eggs with a tint of copper). http://www.chickenchatter.org

3. Hatchery Chicks or Eggs. Try to find one in your area of the country, please, as chicks or eggs are shipped to you by mail or other carrier. Most hatcheries have order size minimums. Examples are McMurray Hatchery in Iowa, http://www.mcmurrayhatchery.com , Mt. Healthy Hatchery in Ohio http://www.mthealthy.com/ , and Ideal Poultry in Texas http://www.ideal-poultry.com/ . I do not have experience ordering from hatcheries and therefore I cannot endorse any of these places. Here is a directory of many more, sorted by online popularity. http://www.top20sites.com/Top-Poultry-Hatcheries-Sites

My Other Publications, all available on Amazon.com
(Click my author name on Amazon to see up to date titles)

1. Backyard Chickens for Beginners: Getting the Best Chickens, Choosing Coops, Feeding and Care, and Beating City Chicken Laws

Description from Amazon:
Excellent booklet for beginners on how to start a backyard mini-flock of 2-4 chickens and get fresh eggs every day. Written by the author of the best-selling Fresh Food From Small Spaces book, a former columnist for Urban Farm magazine. (Updated 2012 Version)

Topics include:
• Fresh Eggs Every Day
• How Much Space Do You Need?
• Building or Buying a Coop
• Feeders, Waterers, Nesting Boxes, and Roosts
• Getting Chicks or Chickens
• Feeding Your Chickens
• Tips for Cold Climates
• Health and Safety
• Dealing with Neighbors, City Chicken Laws, and Other Challenges
• Resources: Everything You Need!

2. How to Grow Potatoes: Planting and Harvesting Organic Food From Your Patio, Rooftop, Balcony, or Backyard Garden (26-page Booklet)

Perfect beginners guide to growing potatoes. This booklet explains how to plant and grow organic potatoes for food in the home garden. Recommended for backyard gardeners and container gardeners with small city-sized yards, patios, balconies, decks, and rooftops.

- Why Grow Potatoes? Six Great Reasons
- Different Kinds of Potatoes (and Where to Get Them)
- Growing in Containers, Raised Beds, and Traditional Rows
- Planting and Hilling Potatoes
- Soil, Fertilizer, and Watering Needs
- Harvesting Potatoes
- Storing Potatoes for Later Use
- *Bonus*: Two Secret Tips for Getting More (and More Delicious) Potatoes

3. **Blueberries in Your Backyard: How to Grow America's Hottest Antioxidant Fruit for Food, Health, and Extra Money**

Description from Amazon:
Perfect blueberry growing guide for beginners. This booklet explains how to plant and grow blueberries in the home garden. Recommended for backyard gardeners with small city-sized yards, patios, balconies, decks, and rooftops. (Updated 2012 version)

Topics include:
- Why Grow Blueberries? Six Great Reasons
- Blueberries for Every Climate (and where to get them)
- Grow Blueberries Almost Anywhere: Doorsteps, Patios, Balconies, Rooftops, and Yards
- Perfect Blueberry Soil (regular garden soil kills them, but they will thrive in this!)
- How to Plant and Grow Blueberries in Raised Beds and Containers
- Feeding, Watering, and Caring for Your Blueberry Bushes
- Making Extra Money Growing Blueberries

3. **Fresh Food From Small Spaces: The Square-Inch Gardener's Guide to Year-Round Growing, Fermenting, and Sprouting,** by R.J. Ruppenthal (Chelsea Green Publishing 2008).
This book covers small space gardening, fermenting (yogurt, kefir, sauerkraut, and kimchi), sprouting, plus chickens for eggs and bees for honey. Over 20,000 people have read this book, which helps beginners learn what they can grow in small urban spaces, such as apartments, condominiums, townhouses, and small homes. Many readers have been motivated to try new things and grow some food where they did not believe they could before reading this. The book is a broad overview, so it does not have a fine level of detail.

Author Info

R.J. Ruppenthal is a licensed attorney and college professor in California who has a passion for growing and raising some of his own food. He regularly writes and blogs about fruit and vegetable gardening, growing food in small urban spaces, sustainability, and raising backyard chickens. On occasion, he even puts his degrees to use and writes something about law or government. You can follow his blogs at http://backyardcvf.blogspot.com or on his Amazon Author's Page here: http://www.amazon.com/R.J.-Ruppenthal/e/B00852ZTT2/ref=ntt_athr_dp_pel_1.

Image attributions

Photos are property of the author or public domain images, except for the following.

Flickr, www.flickr.com
Ameraucana 1, Will Merydith
Australorp hen, Just Chaos
Delaware; Red Sex Links, Linda N.
Marans hen, hardworkinghippy
Plymouth Rock, thomas pix
Rainbow 1, bokeh burger
Rainbow 2, Bob Doran
RIR chick, tquiddle
RIR hens, sammydavisdog
Sussex, owlmonkey

Can Stock Photo, www.canstockphoto.com
Cover
Brahmas 1 and 2
Gold Laced Wyandotte
Silkie 2

Kippen Encyclopedie, www.kippenencyclopedie.nl
Cubalaya hen

Wikimedia Commons, http://commons.wikimedia.org
Australorp chick, gina pina
Marans eggs, Abrahami
Orpingtons, Outback hens
White Crested Black Polish, Joe Mabel
Serama rooster, Nurhafizah Andullah
Serama hen, BrianWI
Silkie 1,Benjamint444
Turken, Demontux
White Leghorns, Geri Glastra

23215063R10027

Made in the USA
Lexington, KY
01 June 2013